SHORESPEARE

By Leslie Tanner

BLACK BOX THEATRE PUBLISHING

Copyright© 2013 by Leslie Tanner
ALL RIGHTS RESERVED
CAUTION: Professionals and amateurs are hereby warned that
Shorespeare (Small Cast Version)
is subject to a royalty. It is fully protected under the copyright laws
of the United States of America, the British Commonwealth,
including Canada, and all other countries of the Copyright Union.

All rights, including professional, amateur, motion
picture, recitation, lecturing, public reading, radio broadcasting,
television and the rights of translation into foreign languages
are strictly reserved. The right to photocopy scripts or videotape
performances can be granted only by the author. In some cases,
the author may choose to allow this, provided permission has
been requested prior to the production. No alterations, deletions
or substitutions may be made to the work without the
written permission of the author.

All publicity material must contain the author"s name,
as the sole author of the work. By producing this play you give the
author and BLACK BOX THEATRE PUBLISHING
the right to use any publicity material including pictures, programs
and posters generated from the production.

To order additional copies of the script, or
to request performance rights, please contact us at
wwwblackboxtheatrepublishing.com

ISBN 978-0615809915

Printed in the United States of America.

Cast

TONI
CLEO
SHAKESPEARE
CUPID
PIXIE 1
PIXIE 2
PIXIE 3
CONFUCIUS
CHARLES PONZI
CARNY
LEONARDO DA VINCI
FIDO
NAPOLEAN
SALLY SMUTHERS
PUCK

Character Notes

The roles are gender neutral besides Toni and Cleo. Since this is based on a Shakespeare play, switching the genders of the historical figures or any of the others would be appropriate. The historical figures can be doubled as well. More pixies can be added as necessary. Also, carnival goers can be added throughout the boardwalk scenes.

Setting

The scenes take place at the Jersey Shore at the seaside and a boardwalk. The stage can be bare and the use of acting blocks and light changes can help set the different scenes. An added backdrop of a carnival or whatever seems appropriate can be used.

SCENE 1

AT RISE: TONI and CLEO are in a frozen pose of longing for each other. Church bells are ringing. SHAKESPEARE appears.

SHAKESPEARE
Two sweethearts from fair New Jersey, is where our play begins.

SOUND: Church bells fade.

CLEO
Yo, Toni!

TONI
Yo, Cleo!

CLEO
It's my birthday!

TONI
And we're gonna party!

CLEO
Like, it's my birthday!

TONI and CLEO dance.

SHAKESPEARE
Sweethearts sworn into youthful love, whose haste to marry plagues their ways.

CLEO
My heart is pumpin' and my toes a tinglin'.

TONI
My gold tooth is rattling and my chest hair is growin'.

TONI and CLEO stop dancing.

CLEO
I'm eighteen. Now I can get a tattoo that says Toni and dot the "i" with a rose.

TONI
Well I was thinking, now that you're 18, well, I just thought. (pause) Cleo, let's get hitched!

CLEO
Oh, Toni! You're all I ever wanted. I even got my nails done extra special for you tonight. Oh, but what will my parent's say?

TONI
Don't ya worry Cleo! I got ya covered. I got three jobs, a swag haircut, and check out these abs!

CLEO
Oh, Toni! You're so hot!

TONI
I've arranged for the magistrate to meet us at the boardwalk tonight.

CLEO
As long as we are back for my curfew at midnight.

TONI
After tonight, I will be in charge of your curfew.

TONI and CLEO exit.

SHAKESPEARE
Thou seest? These naïve nymphs, whose words are pained by a terrible accent. They were bound to elope, that moonlit night at the Jersey shore. But fate would have it that death would arrive at those garbage filled sands. To the nunnery or death!

CUPID
(Running in.)
You cankerblossom!

SHAKESPEARE
Cupid? What brings you forth?

CUPID
You pea! You acorn!

SHAKESPEARE
Get you gone, you dwarf! You're interrupting my play.

CUPID
Enough of your tragedies and foul papers, Shakespeare. It's so 1595. No one's going to listen to you anymore. You need a modern Shakespeare story. One with less death and destruction. And well, we can't really understand what you are saying. It's all texting and cyberspacing down there. These two Jersey sweethearts are your perfect pitch.

SHAKESPEARE
Everyone does despise me these days. They think I'm so boring.

CUPID
Their love is spawned by passion, their minds are full of moos and they're from Jersey!

SHAKESPEARE
Aye, it's a perfect recipe for a modern Shakespeare play. It's going be hard not to kill them.

CUPID
Twist in the absurd instead of the drama. Think of it as, ...kinda like Shakespeare and Jersey shore mixed together.

SHAKESPEARE
We'll call it Shakeshore.

CUPID
Shakeshore? Shoreshake.

SHAKESPEARE
Shoreshake. No. WE will call it...Shorespeare.

CUPID
Okay, whatever. All I'm saying is at least give them a chance at love. Show them what it's like to be married these days. Maybe they'll change their mind and decide that love can wait.

SHAKESPEARE
Then I can kill them?

CUPID
No!

SHAKESPEARE
So what do you propose we do?

CUPID
Write Shakespeare! Write the Course of True Love like it's 2013.

SHAKESPEARE
Four lessons it shall be.

CUPID
The first shall be the Zen of Snoring. One must be able to enure their husband's snoring if marriage is to last.

SHAKESPEARE
Then, how to tell White Lies. I'm good at that.

CUPID
How to Multitask.

SHAKESPEARE
Accepting Shortcomings, shall be the last.

CUPID
Snoring, white lies, multitasking, and accepting shortcomings. Awesome!

SHAKESPEARE
Now fetch your pixies, begone this way, and when the moonlight dangles upon the shore of Jersey, shall the Course of True Love begin for Toni and Cleo. This Jersey things gonna be rough.

CUPID
Pixies won't be happy with this one. They were supposed to have two weeks vacation.

SHAKESPEARE
Thou goatish dewberry, I need your help with this play.

CUPID
Thou logger headed flap-dragon.

SHAKESPEARE
You need to stop me from killing off these Jersey folk.

CUPID
Oh, right.

SHAKESPEARE
Just be on your way. The moon is near rising.

CUPID
I still think you're a logger headed flap-dragon.

SHAKESPEARE
Begone, I say.

CUPID
Remember Shakespeare that the course of love never did run smooth.

SCENE 2

CUPID
Pixies! We've got a job to do.

PIXIES enter.

CUPID
You're going to the Jersey Shore.

PIXIE 1
Really?! The Jersey shore?

PIXIE 2
Those guidos scare me.

PIXIE 3
Yeah, what's up with their tans?

PIXIE 1
Are we gonna get a bonus?

CUPID.
We'll work something out later. All you have to do is sprinkle your pixie dust on the sand. It will make Toni fall asleep and the Zen Master appear, for their first lesson on snoring.

PIXIE 2
Can it be Bruce Lee?

CUPID
He has to be some kind of historical figure, like Confucious. Shakespeare wants to add history into this story.

PIXIE 3
Maybe he can talk like Bruce Lee.

CUPID

Perhaps.

PIXIE 1

When are we done?

CUPID

After lesson four.

ALL PIXIES

Arrgghhhhh!!!

> CUPID exits. The PIXIES sprinkle pixie dust on the sand.

ALL PIXIES

Magic. Magic. Magic spell. We hope you work.

> PIXIES fade into background. TONI enters. HE flexes into the moonlit water, gradually falling asleep. CLEO runs on.

CLEO

Yo, Toni! It's my birthday!
(SHE notices HIM sleeping.)
What have you this? Sleeping? You spongy beef-witted measle. Wake up! Toni! Yo, Toni! Oh, it's no use. I will just lie right here until he awakes.

> SHE falls asleep.

ALL PIXIES
(Unenthusiastically.)
Hooray magic.

PIXIE 2

Can I get a whoop?

PIXIE 1 and 3

Whoop! Whoop!

> PIXIES exit. Silence building into TONI snoring. CLEO hits HIM. Silence. TONI snores. CLEO hits HIM again. Silence. TONI snores and snores and CLEO keeps hitting HIM over and over again.

CLEO

Stop snoring, you unmuzzled flap-mouthed horn-beast!

> MUSIC: Chinese music plays.
> CONFUCIUS enters and bows over CLEO.

CONFUCIUS

(Bows.)

Konichiwa.

CLEO.

(Startled from HER sleep)

Konichiwhat?

CONFUCIUS

It's like a finger pointing away at the moon. If you stare at the finger you miss all of the heavenly glory.

CLEO

Oh master of the kung fu, teach me some moves to stop Toni's snoring.

CONFUCIUS

I am Confucius. I am not a fighter. I am a thinker. Never stir hand or foot in defiance. You must cultivate your Ren.

CLEO

Is that some kind of new hair product?

CONFUCIUS
Ren is compassion-to love others. So, you must be one with Toni's snoring.

CLEO
I'll be one with this kung fu move.

> CLEO tries some kung fu on TONI which makes HIM snore even louder.

CLEO
It's no use. How can I marry someone whose going to snore in my ear every night.

CONFUCIUS
Come here, my friend. Empty your mind, be formless.

> CLEO poses in an odd shape.

CONFUCIUS
Shapeless, like water. Be water.

> CLEO starts to wiggle and flow like water. TONI still snores.

CONFUCIUS
Now, bow to your opponent.

> CLEO bows to CONFUCIUS instead of TONI. CONFUCIUS slaps HER in the head.

CLEO
Ow!

CONFUCIUS
Never take your eye off your opponent. Try again.

> CLEO bows looking at TONI.

CONFUCIUS
Good. Now look into your mind.
>(Pause.)
What is it saying?

CLEO
>(Sighs.)
I've got to get extensions done to this hair. I better call Niki to fix this nail. What happened to my bronzer? My father's gonna kill me when he finds out I've married Toni.
>(Yelling.)
Stop snoring!

CONFUCIUS
Silence! Empty your mind. See each thought as a floating cloud in the sky. Do not give any emotion to your thoughts. Try again.
>(Pause.)
What's it saying now?

CLEO
Be like finger. Flow like...
>(TONI snores.)
..snoring. That's all I hear. I swear.

CONFUCIUS
My friend, defeat is not defeat unless accepted as a reality in your own mind. Let this not defeat you! The Buddha can clean toilets for many hours without complaining.

CLEO
I sure don't ever want to be a Buddha.

CONFUCIUS
My friend, take from your teacher this lesson of Zen, place it dear to your heart, and one day, you might understand. Namaste.

> MUSIC: Chinese music plays.
> CONFUCIUS bows. CONFUCIUS exits.
> MUSIC: Chinese music fades. CLEO goes over to TONI who is still snoring. SHE karate chops HIM.

TONI
(Awakening.)
Ow! What was that for?

CLEO
You're a snoring fool. Get up!

TONI
Man, I zonked out. I was dreaming about this wicked kung fu pixie fight.

CLEO
Come on, Toni, we need to get to the boardwalk to meet the magistrate.

> THEY start to exit as SHAKESPEARE enters.

SHAKESPEARE.
Do not haste in this timely decision.

TONI
Who's this guy?

CLEO
Got me?

SHAKESPEARE
I'm a modern poet, named Shakespeare.

CLEO
I think I've heard that name before. Were you a guest on the "Bad Girls Club"?

SHAKESPEARE
No, but that sounds intriguing. I am here to tell you that before you elope, you must show that you can endure the tribulations of marriage.

CLEO
Did my Dad send you here?

TONI
Come on Cleo! This guy is a freak!

CLEO and TONI exit.

SHAKESPEARE.
(Calling off.)
Cupid! They're ready for the next lesson.

CUPID enters.

CUPID
Thanks for holding them up. I lost the pixies in the nightclub. They should be at the boardwalk by now.

SHAKESPEARE.
Let the second lesson begin.

CUPID and SHAKESPEARE exit.

SCENE 3

AT RISE: On the boardwalk. Pixies are in a photo booth posing for pictures. SOUND: Beep. Beep.

PIXIE 1

Say Jersey!

ALL PIXIES

Jersey!

SOUND: Beep. LIGHTS: Flash.

PIXIE 2

Party face!

SOUND: Beep. Beep.

ALL PIXIES

Partay!

SOUND: Beep. LIGHTS: Flash.

PIXIE 3

Fabuliscious!

SOUND: Beep. Beep.

ALL PIXIES

Fabuliscious!

SOUND: Beep. LIGHTS: Flash.

PIXIE 1
Now hurry up and spread the pixie dust.

PIXIE 2 spreads the pixie dust.

> PIXIE 3

Hurry up. Here they come.

> PIXIES exit. CLEO and TONI enter towards photo booth.

> CLEO

Toni, look it's a photo booth. We need to take some photos for our wedding album.

> TONI

Sure thing, hot pants!

> THEY enter the photo booth. TONI flexes.

> CLEO.

Stop that.

> SOUND: Beep. Beep.

> CLEO.

Be serious.

> LIGHTS: Flash. CHARLES PONZI poses between THEM.

> PONZI

Ciao!

> TONI and CLEO scream.

> TONI

Yo, dude, what are you doing?

> PONZI

My name is Carlo Pietro Giovanni Guglielmo Tebaldo Ponzi.

CLEO
What did he just say?

PONZI
Just call me Ponzi, or Charles. Whatever you prefer.

TONI
Listen dude….

PONZI
I was sent here to teach you how to tell white lies. It's one of the most essential elements to keeping each other happy in marriage.

CLEO
Not this again. Did my Dad send you here?

PONZI
White lies build confidence in marriage. If you want to master love, you must master white lies, and, well, I'm pretty much the master at that.

TONI
I'm not really feelin' ya.

PONZI
I've learned how to turn two dollars into millions. In 1903 I arrived in the United States with only two dollars and fifty cents. At forty-two I was selling vegetables, but in eight months time I was making millions, all by telling little white lies. Some may call me a fraud, but I'm really just a quick-witted genius.

TONI
All right, I'm feeling ya.

PONZI
We're gonna play a little game…..for money. For each white lie you can tell I will give you one dollar. If you tell the truth then you give me five dollars. So, let's get started. Toni, tell Cleo where you were last Thursday night.

TONI
I was out with the boys…..oh crap.

CLEO
What!? You said you were working late. We were gonna go to the movies.

PONZI
Zero for one. That'll be five dollars.
    (TONI hands HIM money.)
Try again. Cleo pretend you just got back from the hair salon.

> CLEO exits, then enters with HER hair flipped out.

CLEO
Yo Toni, how do you like my blowout?

TONI
It's smokin'. It's so fluffy and flatters your…..nose.

CLEO
What's wrong with my nose?

TONI
Nothing. It's like a charming little…troll.

CLEO
A troll!? Well your nose is a lumpish weather-bitten barnacle.

PONZI
That'll be ten more dollars.

> TONI hands over money. SOUND: TONI'S phone rings.

TONI
Yo, how ya doin? Let me call you right back.

CLEO
Who was that?

TONI
Oh…ah….that was Paulie.

CLEO
What's he doing calling you? I thought he was in the slammer?

> PONZI snatches phone.

PONZI
Actually it was Snooki. Hand over the money.

> TONI hands over money.

CLEO
Oh fughedaboudit!

> SHE exits.

TONI
Oh fughedaboudit?

PONZI
Fughedaboudit!

TONI

Fughedaboudit?

PONZI

You should never tell a lady the truth about certain things. It only creates problems. One day Toni, you will understand.

>TONI exits.

PONZI

Ciao!

>PONZI exits. SHAKESPEARE enters.

SHAKESPEARE

Two sweethearts torn apart from truthful words. Cleo lost in despair on the boardwalk of the Jersey shore.
>(CLEO enters.)

Her pace, dismal and paltry.
>(Calling off to TONI.)

Anon, Toni!
>(TONI enters.)

Leap long strides to win the heart of your future bride, Before thy death swallows thee.

>TONI leaps long strides towards CLEO.
>THEY freeze. CUPID enters.

CUPID
>(Sarcastically.)

Way to keep it positive Bard!

SHAKESPEARE

They have already failed two lessons of the course.

CUPID

There's still time for redemption.

SHAKESPEARE
I've already ordered the poison from Friar Lawrence.

CUPID
Well send it back. This is a course on love, not destruction.

SHAKESPEARE
Are they not one and the same? Destruction. Love? No longer can I endure this stupidity.

CUPID
Think of this as a folly. A folly of love. One that flitters for a little while and then just flickers out. Like a midsummer night's dream.

SHAKESPEARE
More like a late summer evening's nightmare.

CUPID
Well, they have two more lessons. Let's see what folly we can mix up.

SHAKESPEARE
Get ye gone, Cupid, and gather thy pixies for their lesson on multiplying tasks. They are sure to fail. Then to the nunnery or death!

CUPID
Oh, Bard.

THEY exit.

SCENE 4

AT RISE: PIXIES are on a Ferris wheel at the boardwalk.
MUSIC: Carnival music plays.

PIXIE 3
Weeeee! Up we go. Whoop! Whoop!

PIXIE 2
Whoop! Whoop!

> Ferris wheel stops at the top. MUSIC: Carnival music fades.

PIXIE 1
(Breathing in,)
Ahhhhh! Smell that Jersey air. It's quite fresh on top of this ferris wheel.

PIXIE 2
It's like fish and garbage.

PIXIE 3
With a twist of fruity cologne.

PIXIE 2
Look there's Cleo and Toni.

PIXIE 1
They're talking smack.

> CLEO enters followed by TONI.

TONI
Cleo!

CLEO
Toni, how could you? Snooki?

TONI
Come on Cleo! Ya know she's crazy. Fughedaboudit.

CLEO
You're a villainous toad-spotted liar!

TONI
I just didn't want to hurt your feelings.

CLEO
You're a maggot-pie.

TONI
Snooki is nothing to me. She's just trying to split us up.

CLEO
Pignut!

CLEO and TONI freeze.

PIXIE 3
Oh snap.

PIXIE 2
She told him.

PIXIE 3
Go Cleo! It's your birthday!

PIXIE 2 and 3
And we're gonna party, like it's your birthday!

PIXIE 1
Stop you two. Throw the pixie dust over them. Let's see how they fare.

> PIXIE 2 and 3 throw the pixie dust over THEM. CLEO and TONI unfreeze and there is a sudden shift in THEIR demeanor.

CLEO
Toni, my sweetheart.

TONI
It's time to go meet the magistrate. It's almost midnight.

CLEO
Let's go for a ride on the ferris wheel first?

TONI
Anything for you, hot pants.

> TONI and CLEO walk towards ferris wheel as the PIXIES ride down. CARNY enters to let PIXIES off ride.

PIXIE 3
Weee! Down we go.

PIXIE 2
Can I get a whoop!

PIXIE 3
Whoop!

PIXIE 1
Enough with the fist pumping you two. The Jersey shore has demented your brains.

CARNY
Hope you enjoyed the ride. Exit to the left.

PIXIE 3
See you on the flip side.

PIXIES exit.

CARNY

Step right up! Only two tickets to ride. Come see the sights of the Jersey shore and make out under the stars.

TONI
(Handing over tickets.)
That's what I'm talkin' about.

CLEO
(To Carny.)
Is this ride going to frizz my hair?

CARNY
(Shoves THEM into the ride.)
Buckle up! Enjoy the ride.

MUSIC: Carnival music.

CLEO

Oh, Toni this is so amazing. Soon we will be married and nestled in a house at the Jersey shore.

SOUND: Sounds of a machine breaking.
MUSIC: Carnival music stops.

CLEO

Oh snap!

TONI
(To Carny.)
Yo! What's goin' on?

CARNY
Oh geeze, not the motor again.

CLEO
(To TONI.)

Are we stuck?

CARNY

Ladies and gentlemen, the Ferris wheel is broke. Please be patient while we fix the problem. Stay buckled in your seat with your arms and legs inside.

TONI
(Standing.)
You gotta be kiddin' me.

CARNY

This is not a joke sir. Please stay seated with your buckle fastened.

CLEO
(Pulling TONI down.)
Sit, Toni, sit.

TONI

Don't talk to me like I'm a dog.

CLEO

I thought you liked it when I talked dog? Woof. Woof.

CARNY
(Calling off.)
Leonardo! Yo Da Vinci! We've got a problem here.

TONI
(Standing.)
I'll give you a problem.

CARNY

Sir, sit down.

CLEO
(Pulling TONI down.)
It's almost midnight, Toni. We're never gonna get hitched.

> LEONARDO enters.

CARNY
Da Vinci, can you fix this ride before that freak jumps off?

TONI
Who you calling a freak?

LEONARDO
Are you kidding me? I invented this thing. One of my many inventions. Hand me the pliers.

> CARNY hands over pliers.

LEONARDO
Well, I invented this too. Your world wouldn't exist if it weren't for me. I was the mastermind behind bridges, helicopters, parachutes, automobiles, tanks, and machine guns. Most people remember me for my masterpiece paintings The Last Supper and the Mona Lisa.

> SOUND: Breaking machine noises. PIXIES fly in and throw pixie dust on CLEO and TONI.

ALL PIXIES
(Unenthused.)
Magic. Magic. Magic spell. We hope you work.

> PIXIES exit. TONI and CLEO tumble out of the Ferris wheel. CARNY marks off area with hazard tape.

CLEO
Oh no! I chipped another nail.

TONI
What's going on here dude?

CLEO
Toni it's almost midnight.

TONI and CLEO start to exit.

LEONARDO
Not so fast. We've got some work to do.

TONI
Out of my way you tottering tickle-brained bugbear.

CARNY
Sorry sir. No crossing the orange tape.

LEONARDO
If you want this lady's hand in marriage you are going to have to pass this lesson. I will fix this ferris wheel while you conduct a multitude of tasks.

CLEO
Did my Dad send you here?

LEONARDO
And you my lady will have to do the same. You both shall become masters at multitasking.

CLEO
That's easy. I always paint my nails and watch Bad Girls Club at the same time.

LEONARDO
Let's see how you perform. Carny, get them their task lists.

CARNY exits.

LEONARDO
I am the master of multitasking, but I prefer to be called a Renaissance man. I am a scientist, artist, inventor, architect, astronomer, botanist, chemist, engineer, and musician all at the same time.

CARNY enters with task lists and props-leash, rake, kitchen appliance and phone bill.

LEONARDO
In marriage you have to be able to balance a variety of tasks all at once. Toni you're first. Carny here, will hand you each tasks, as he deems necessary.

SHAKESPEARE and CUPID enter in the distance.

LEONARDO
Let's start off by walking Fido, your future dog.

CARNY hands TONI a leash.

CARNY
Here Fido. Come on. Good boy.

FIDO enters and sits next to TONI. TONI tries to put on leash, but FIDO runs around stage in circles. TONI finally captures HIM and puts on the leash. HE walks the dog.

LEONARDO
Time to rake the leaves.

CARNY hands TONI the rake. FIDO thinks it's a toy.

FIDO
Woof. Woof. Arrrggghhh.

TONI.
No Fido. Stop it. Bad dog.

>   THEY play tug of war with the rake.

LEONARDO
Time to fix the toaster. (NOTE: Or any other appliance.)

>   CARNY hands over appliance.

CARNY
Here you go.

LEONARDO
(Handing over pliers.)
You'll probably need these too.

>   TONI attempts to fix appliance while still playing tug of war with FIDO.

FIDO
Woof. Woof. Arggghhh.

TONI
Sit, Fido, sit. Bad dog.

LEONARDO
Time to pay your cell phone bill.

>   CARNY hands over phone bill. TONI already has HIS phone in HIS pocket.

CARNY
Here's the number.

> TONI dials phone while balancing dog, rake, and appliance. SOUND: A recording is heard.

RECORDING
Please be patient while we transfer your call. Your call is important to us.

> MUSIC: Bad elevator music. FIDO sees something in the distance and jumps, knocking over TONI.

TONI
Oh fughedaboudit!

> FIDO runs off.

SHAKESPEARE
What a mangled fool-born nut-hook.

CUPID
Chill Bard.

CLEO
That was so funny, I almost peed my pants.

TONI
Whatever.

LEONARDO
Let's see how you perform.

SHAKESPEARE
Down with the dame.

> CARNY exits with TONI'S props. CARNY enters with CLEO'S props-nail polish, brush, hairspray, basket of mismatched socks, and calling list.

CUPID
Enough Bard.

LEONARDO
First we start with your nails, since that seems to be most important to you.

> CARNY hands over nail polish to CLEO.

CLEO
Hot pink is so my color.

> SHE paints HER nails.

LEONARDO.
And your hair of course.

> CARNY hands over brush and hairspray to CLEO, who paints HER nails and does HER hair.

LEONARDO
Don't forget about Toni's laundry.

> CARNY throws a pile of mismatched socks over CLEO.

CLEO
Toni these stink like maggot pies.

> CLEO sorts socks, paints nails, and does HER hair.

LEONARDO
Be sure to make all your phone calls.

CUPID
(Calling off.)
Pixies, your on!

> CARNY calling list to CLEO. CLEO already has HER phone in pocket. PIXIES pose around CLEO to take the calls. CLEO dials phone, while continuing with nails, hair, and socks.

PIXIE 1
Thanks for calling Sun Tan City. We make you shine like gold.

CLEO
I'd like to come in on Monday around five.

PIXIE 1
Is that for a spray tan or booth?

CLEO
Both. And make it a double.

PIXIE 1
I need your Sun Tan City member number please.

CLEO
I can't find it right now. Can I call you back?

> CLEO hangs up and calls second number.

PIXIE 2
Casa de Pasta, home of the spicy meatballs.

CLEO
I'd like to make a reservation for two.

PIXIE 2
Please wait.
> (Pause.)

Please wait.
> (Pause.)

Please wait.
> (Pause.)

Casa de Pasta, home of the spicy meatballs.

CLEO
I'd like to make a reservation.

PIXIE 2
Please wait.

> CLEO hangs up, dials third number, while still doing HER nails, hair, and socks.

PIXIE 3
Omg Cleo you'll never believe what Joey did, and Tara went ballistic. They were screamin' and fighten' and oh did you hear about that new show where they take famous people and put them in a trailer park for a week? You gotta see this new outfit I got for Friday night at the club. It's sooooo awesome. You're gonna love it.

> Overlapping.

PIXIE 2
Please wait.

PIXIE 1
Sun Tan City. We make you shine like gold.

PIXIE 3
You're gonna love it.

PIXIE 2
Please wait.

PIXIE 1
Sun Tan City. We make you shine like gold.

PIXIE 3
You're gonna love it.

CLEO
(Hanging up.)
Oh fughedaboudit!

PIXIES run off.

TONI
Not so easy right?

MUSIC: Carnival music. CARNY clears tape.

LEONARDO
Ahah! The Ferris wheel is working.

CARNY
Nice work Da Vinci.

LEONARDO
Ah yes, the art of multitasking can create magnificent masterpieces. As for the two of you, well, you have a ways to go.

CLEO
Toni it's almost midnight!

TONI and CLEO exit.

CARNY
Can you tell me about that underwater breathing apparatus you designed?

LEONARDO and CARNY exit.

SCENE 5

AT RISE: CUPID and SHAKESPEARE come downstage.

SHAKESPEARE
Oh grim-look'd night! Oh night with hue so black! Oh wicked curs'd love. Oh fools!

CUPID
Oh Shakespeare! There's no time for your monologues that go on and on for pages. Cleo's curfew is near and there's still one more lesson.

SHAKESPEARE
Ah yes, the comings of short, which will show utter failure.

CUPID
You mean shortcomings?

SHAKESPEARE
Oh failings! Oh flaws! Come down unto these two fools of love.

CUPID
It's obvious that they have flaws, but they need to be able to accept each other's flaws if they want to get married.

SHAKESPEARE
Then let the games begin.

SHAKESPEARE exits.

CUPID
(Calling off.)
Pixies! It's target practice time!

> PIXIES enter, each holding a bull's eye target.

PIXIE 1
What's our job this time?

CUPID
Sprinkle your pixie dust at this carnival game and spread yourselves out into the crowd. You will be the targets for Toni and Cleo.

PIXIE 2
I'd rather eat dirt.

PIXIE 3
Or get a spray tan.

CUPID
This is the last lesson of the course of true love. Then you can get back to your vacation.

PIXIE 1
And what about our bonus?

CUPID
We'll work that out later. Now hurry.

> PIXIES sprinkle pixie dust.

ALL PIXIES.
Magic. Magic. Magic spell. We hope you work.

> MUSIC: Carnival Music. PIXIES run into audience with targets. CUPID brings block or stool down center stage and places a basket of nerf balls. NAPOLEON BONAPARTE enters holding an oversized stuffed animal.

NAPOLEON.
Step right up to Napoleon's revenge. Only three tokens.

TONI and CLEO enter. MUSIC: Carnival music fades.

NAPOLEON
Monsieur, Madame. Only three tokens. Seek your revenge.

CLEO.
Oh Toni, win me that bear. (NOTE: Or whatever animal chosen.) It's so adorable.

TONI
But Cleo, we're gonna be late for the magistrate.

NAPOLEON
(Shouting.)
Play the game you saucy swag-bellied scut!

TONI
You talkin' to me?

NAPOLEON
I said play the game you SAUCY SWAG-BELLIED SCUT!

TONI
(Handing over tokens.)
I can beat this game any day you midget.

NAPOLEON
Don't call me SHORT, or I will KILL you. I'm the cruelest BULLY you will ever meet. I conquered all the European nations and usurped the French throne, for I am NAPOLEAN BONAPARTE. A short MEGOLOMANIAC!

TONI
Let's play the game Bonaparte. What do I gotta do?

NAPOLEON
Three tokens. Three shots. You see those targets out there?

PIXIE 1

Whoop!

PIXIE 2

Whoop!

PIXIE 3

Whoop!

TONI

I think they were in my dream earlier tonight.

NAPOLEON

If you miss, one of your shortcomings will be revealed.

CLEO

What are shortcomings?

NAPOLEON

(Shouts.)

FAILINGS. And each of you has them, just like me. Let us begin. Step right up.

> NAPOLEON hands TONI three nerf balls. TONI throws them, hitting two and missing one.

ALL PIXIES

Sucka!

CLEO

Hey, no one talks to Toni that way except for me.

NAPOLEON

Sally Smuthers will you please reveal Toni's first flaw to the audience.

>   SALLY SMUTHERS enters holding a sign
>   that says "WORKING OUT".

CLEO
Are we on T.V.? I've always wanted to be on T.V.

NAPOLEON
And you young lady get to choose whether to LIVE WITH or LIVE WITHOUT.

>   SALLY SMUTHERS holds up two signs.
>   One says "LIVE WITH" and the other says
>   "LIVE WITHOUT".

CLEO
And then we get the bear?

NAPOLEON
Then you get the bear. And perhaps even get married. But, can you both live with each other's shortcomings? We will soon find out.

CLEO
Do I still get the bear even if we can't get married?

NAPOLEON
    (Shouts)
NO! Now begin.

>   SALLY SMUTHERS brings on a large
>   dumbbell.

NAPOLEON
Now show us your stuff.

>   TONI does a crazy workout out session.

TONI
This is my situation. Gettin' shredded yeah!

> MUSIC: Work out music. TONI'S jam.
> TONI does dead lifts with dumbbell.

TONI
Oooh. Ooooh. Yeah. Yeah. Bakin' some hams. This is how you get ripped fast.
> (TONI does push ups.)

Ooooh. Ooooh. Yeah, baby! Gettin' ripped bro!
> (TONI does bench presses with dumbbell on block.)

Yeah. Yeah. Yeah. This is how I roll. Fist pumpin' baby!
> (TONI fist pumps and makes unusual facial expressions.)

Oooh. Yeah. Oooh. Yeah.
> (MUSIC: Music fades.)

I'm gettin' ripped like Hercules, cause this is my situation. I'm cut bro. Totally shredded.

NAPOLEON
> (Shouts.)

Cleo!

CLEO
> (Startled.)

Ahhhhh!

NAPOLEAN
What do you think of Toni's workout session?

CLEO
I'm not sure. It's a little scary.

NAPOLEAN
Are you gonna LIVE WITH or LIVE WITHOUT?

> PIXIES hum a game show theme song from audience. SALLY approaches CLEO with signs.

CLEO
(Holding up LIVE WITHOUT sign.)
I'm so sorry Toni. I don't wanna ever see you workout again.

TONI
Who's gonna protect you from those pignuts at the club?

NAPOLEAN
Do you want that bear? Then let's move right along. Step right up.

> CLEO steps up on block. NAPOLEAN hands HER three nerf balls. CLEO throws ball at PIXIE 1 and misses.

PIXIE 1
You prissy poopy-pants.

> CLEO throws at PIXIE 2 and misses.

PIXIE 2
You throw like a grandma.

> CLEO throws at PIXIE 3 and misses.

PIXIE 3
You foot-licker!

> PIXIES exit back of audience.

CLEO
What did you just call me? Did I win the bear?

NAPOLEON
Let's bring out your shortcomings. Sally Smuthers please reveal Cleo's flaw.

> SALLY holds up a sign saying, "SELFISIH, BOORISH, LOATHSOME, RUDE, CLASSLESS".

NAPOLEON.
Selfish, boorish, loathsome, rude, and classless. Wow! You might have me beat.

CLEO
I'm not sure I know what those words mean.

NAPOLEON
Let's take them into context then. A little role-playing will be quite amusing. Sally Smuthers will you please set up the club.

SALLY
(To audience.)
I need dancers!

PIXIE 2
I wanna dance!

PIXIE 3
Can I get a whoop! Whoop!

> PIXIES 2 and 3 run up on stage.

PIXIE 1
(Following.)
REALLY?!

> SALLY and NAPOLEON.

LIGHTS!

LIGHTS: Light change.

MUSIC! SALLY and NAPOLEON.

MUSIC: Club or dance music.

DANCING! SALLY and NAPOLEON.

SALLY holds up "DANCE" sign. PIXIES dance center stage.

SALLY
(Out to audience.)
Anyone else want to go clubbin'?

SALLY encourages audience members to come and dance. They join the PIXIES center stage. CARNY appears and places a marquee in front of dancers. CARNY exits. NAPOLEON guards the entrance.

SALLY
(Holding up signs.)
All you have do is either FREEZE or DANCE!

Once on stage SALLY holds up "DANCE" sign.

CLEO
Oh Toni, let's go clubbin'!

TONI
Anything for you, hot pants! We've got about 5 minutes till we're married.

CLEO.
Quit calling me hot pants. It's so embarrassing.

> TONI and CLEO enter marquee.
> NAPOLEON stops them.

NAPOLEON
(Shouts.)
WAIT IN LINE!

CLEO
What line? There is no line.

NAPOLEON
There is now.

CLEO
Toni, do something. Stop standing there like a puking pickle-fed lout.

TONI
What do you want me to do?

> SALLY SMUTHERS holds up "FREEZE" sign. PIXIES & DANCERS freeze. MUSIC: Club music stops.

CLEO
Punch him out or something.

TONI
(Flexing.)
Nah! I'm not wasting these muscles on that short guy.

NAPOLEON
No one calls me SHORT!

CLEO
(Fighting HER way to the door.)
And no one's gettin' between me and the club.

NAPOLEON
I don't think so, you mewling spleen.

CLEO
Toni, you see how he's talkin' to me?

> TONI is still absorbed in HIS flexing.

CLEO
(To TONI.)
Ugghh!
(To NAPOLEON.)
Let me in the club you short pumped little French guy. I'll trash talk this club until it sizzles and fries.

> SALLY holds up "DANCE" sign. MUSIC: DANCE/CLUB music PIXIES and DANCERS dance.

NAPOLEON
Wow! It's really hoppin' in there. Too bad you have to wait in line.

> CLEO pulls HER hair, spits on HER hand, wipes it on TONI, takes HER shoes off and throws them on the ground.

CLEO
This club is goin' down.

TONI
Cleo, babe, chill.

CLEO
I wanna go clubbin'!

NAPOLEON
Sorry madame, club's closing.

> SALLY SMUTHERS holds up "FREEZE" sign. PIXIES help DANCERS back to their seats. CARNY enters and removes marquee.

NAPOLEON
Ah well, that sure was fun. A little role-playing to get the night going.

CLEO
This is not fun.

NAPOLOEON
Ah yes. Seeing one's shortcomings face to face is a bit revealing. Even harder is accepting other's failings. Well, Toni, are you going to LIVE WITH or LIVE WITHOUT?

> PIXIES hum a game show theme song from audience. SALLY approaches TONI with signs.

TONI
Ummmm…..ummmmm......Live without.

> SALLY holds up sign "LIVE WITHOUT".

CLEO
Did I win the bear?

NAPOLEON
Afraid not, Madame.

> NAPOLEON steps back up on block/stool
> and stands out to audience.

NAPOLEON
Step right up to Napoleon's revenge. Only three tokens.

CLEO
Toni, are we still gonna get married?

> LIGHTS: Fade. TONI and CLEO exit.
> NAPOLEON exits. SHAKESPEARE enters.

SHAKESPEARE
Oh timely day, I wish it were a timely death. Two sweethearts from fair New Jersey torn by failings of preposterous nature. Oh sweaty mule who bakes hams! Oh classless boor with blackened selfishness! To the magistrate I am abound.

> SHAKESPEARE exits.

SCENE 6

>CUPID runs across stage after
>SHAKESPEARE.

CUPID
Bard! Bard! Who will play the magistrate?

>ALL PIXIES run across stage.

ALL PIXIES
Cupid! Cupid! Where's our bonus?

>PIXIES exit. PUCK enters.

PUCK.
Up and down, Up and down.
Through honeysuckles, through bogs of the Great Swamp.
Through insect ingesting plants, through the Pine Barrens.
Sometime a horse I'll be, sometime a bear,
A timber rattlesnake, and eastern tiger swallowtail.
And neigh, and roar, and hiss, and caw, at every turn.
Puck I am. That merry wanderer of the night. A trickster.
A mishievious fellow. But yet the Bard did hire me to be a magistrate at the Jersey Shore.

>Enter TONI and CLEO.

TONI
We're here to get hitched.

CLEO
Are you the magistrate?

PUCK
Sir Puck the magistrate here to tie your vows.

CLEO
Toni, did we bring our vows?

TONI
We don't need no vows, Sir Puck.

PUCK
No vows you say? Well then whatever shall we tie?

CLEO
Maybe you could tie our shirts together.

PUCK
(Aside.)
Cupid is a knavish lad, thus to make poor females mad.
(To TONI and CLEO.)
Shall we sing a wedding song?

What is love? Baby don't hurt me.
Don't hurt me no more.
Oh baby, baby don't hurt me.
Whoa whoa whoa, oooh oooh.

TONI
Hold your tongue!

CLEO
Toni, don't be rude. That was a nice song.

TONI
Can we just get to the "I do" part?

PUCK
I do want a corndog!

CLEO
Me too!

Enter CUPID and SHAKESPEARE.

PUCK
What fellow guests have we here?

CLEO
Toni, it's that guy from the "Bad Girls Club"!

PUCK
Shakespeare, I never knew this side of you.

SHAKESPEARE
Enough Puck!

PUCK
Yes, on with it! Do you Cleo take this sluggish hard-nosed guido to be your awful husband?

CLEO
I do.

PUCK
Do you Toni, take this feather haired bronzed girl to be your awful wife?

TONI
I do.

PUCK
Well, then, you may now kiss the.....

CUPID
Hold it! Sorry to break it to you, but the marriage can't go on.

CLEO
Why not? Toni, do something.

                    TONI
What do ya want me to do?

                    CUPID
You didn't pass the course of true love.

                    CLEO
Oh.

                    SHAKESPEARE
The Zen of Snoring.

                    CUPID and SHAKESPEARE
Failed!

                    SHAKESPEARE
Telling White Lies.

                    CUPID and SHAKESPEARE
Failed!

                    SHAKESPEARE
The Art of Multi-tasking.

                    CUPID and SHAKESPEARE
Failed!

                    SHAKESPEARE
Accepting Shortcomings.

                    CUPID and SHAKESPEARE
Failed!

                    CLEO
Oh, Toni my love! Thou art not my love, I think.

                    TONI
Oh, cherry-lipped Cleo, gettin' hitched is a bad idea, I think.

SHAKESPEARE, PUCK and CUPID
Ya think?

PUCK
Alack, alack pour souls!

SHAKESPEARE
Beshrew my heart.

CLEO
Toni, it's past my curfew. My father's gonna kill you and me both.

TONI and CLEO exit.

PUCK
Farewell friends. Adieu, adieu, adieu.

SHAKESPEARE
By moonshine did lovers think to woo. Sweet youth with speech like a tangled chain. O fates!

LIGHTS: Fade.

THE END

If you have enjoyed this play, please leave a review on

amazon

and

BLACK BOX THEATRE PUBLISHING

NOW AVAILABLE!!!

Poop Happens!" in this send up of all things cowboy!

So, Who Was That Masked Guy Anyway? is the story of Ernie, the grandson of the original Masked Cowboy, a lawman who fought for truth, justice and the cowboy way in the old west. Now that Grandpa is getting on in years he's looking for someone to carry on for him. The only problem? Ernie doesn't know anything about being a cowboy. He's never seen a real cow, he's allergic to milk and to tell the truth he doesn't know one end of a horse from another! So it's off to cowboy school to learn the basics of cowboyology. He'll learn to rope and ride, chew and spit and to develop the perfect "Yee-Haw!". And it's a good thing, because a band of no good outlaws have captured the good people of Gabby Gulch and the President of the United States, Theodore Roosevelt! Now it's up to Ernie and his friends to save the day...but beware, before it's all over, the poop is sure to hit the fans!

NOW AVAILABLE!!!

WANTED: SANTA CLAUS is the story of what happens when a group of department store moguls led by the greedy B. G. Bucks decide to replace Santa Claus with the shiny new "KRINGLE 3000", codenamed...ROBO-SANTA! A new Father Christmas with a titanium alloy outer shell housing a nuclear powered drive train, not to mention a snow white beard and a jolly disposition! These greedy tycoons will stop at nothing to get rid of jolly old St. Nick. That includes framing him for such crimes as purse snatching, tire theft and...oh no...not.....puppy kicking??!! Say it isn't so Santa! Now it's up to Santa's elves to save the day! But Santa's in no shape to take on his stainless steel counterpart! He'll have to train for his big comeback. Enter Mickey, one of the toughest elves of all time! He'll get Santa ready for the big showdown! But it's going to mean reaching deep down inside to find "the eye of the reindeer"!

NOW AVAILABLE!!!

At the edge of the universe sits The Long John Cafe. A place where the average guy and the average "Super" guy can sit and have a cup of coffee and just be themselves...or, someone else if that's what they want. The cafe is populated by iconic figures of the 20th Century, including cowboys, hippies, super heroes and movie stars. They've come to celebrate the end of the old Century and the beginning of tomorrow! That is, if they make it through the night! It seems the evil Dr. McNastiman has other plans for our heroes. Like their total destruction!

NOW AVAILABLE!!!

Why should the boys get to have all the fun?

Jacklyn Sparrow and the Lady Pirates of the Caribbean is our brand new swashbuckling pirate parody complete with bloodthirsty buccaneers in massive sword clanking battle scenes!! A giant wise cracking parrot named Polly!! Crazy obsessions with eye liner!! And just who is Robert, the Dreaded Phylum Porifera??

Of course the whole thing ends with a large celebration where everybody gets down with their bad selves!! It's fun for the whole family in this lampoon of everything you love about pirates!!!

NOW AVAILABLE!!!

"May the Dwarf be with you!"

A wacky take on the classic fairy tale which will have audiences rolling in the floor with laughter!

What happens when you mix an articulate mirror, a conceited queen, a prince dressed in purple, seven little people with personality issues, a basket of kumquats and a little Star Wars for good measure?

Snow White and the Seven Dwarves of the Old Republic!

NOW AVAILABLE!!!

Dear John
An ode to the potty.

"My dreams of thee flow softly.
They enter with tender rush.
The still soft sound which echoes,
When I lower the lid and flush."

They say that porcelain is the best antenna for creativity. At least that's what this cast of young people believe in Dear John: An ode to the potty! The action of this one act play takes place almost entirely behind the doors of five bathroom stalls. This short comedy is dedicated to all those term papers, funny pages and Charles Dickens' novels that have been read behind closed (stall) doors!

Bathroom humor at its finest!

NOW AVAILABLE!!!

Declassified after 40 years!

On December 21, 1970, an impromptu meeting took place between the King of Rock and Roll and the Leader of the Free World.

Elvis Meets Nixon (Operation Wiggle) is a short comedy which offers one possible (and ultimately ridiculous) explanation of what happened during that meeting.

NOW AVAILABLE!!!

Even Adam

**In the beginning, there was a man.
Then there was a woman.
And then there was this piece of fruit...
...and that's when everything went horribly wrong!
Even Adam is a short comedy exploring the relationship
between men and women right from day one.**

**Why doesn't he ever bring her flowers like he used to?
Why doesn't she laugh at his jokes anymore?
And just who is that guy in the red suit?
And how did she convince him to eat that fruit, anyway?**

NOW AVAILABLE!!!

Count Dracula is bored. He's pretty much sucked Transylvania dry, and he's looking for a new challenge. So it's off to New York, New York! The Big Apple! The town that never sleeps...that'll pose a challenge for sure.
Dracula purchases The Carfax Theatre and decides to put on a big, flashy Broadway show...

THE DRACULA SPECTACULA!

Of course the Theatre just happens to be across the street from Dr. Seward's Mental Hospital where people have been mysteriously dying since The Count moved in.
Just a coincidence?
The play features a large cast of zany characters and is equal parts horror story and Broadway show spoof!

NOW AVAILABLE!!!

THE FOUR PRESIDENTS examines the lives and characters of four of the most colorful personalities to hold the office. Much of the dialogue comes from the Presidents' own words.

THE FARMER WHO WOULD BE KING presents George Washington through his own words, and the words of his biographer Mason Locke Weems. Was the father of our country a simple farmer who answered the call of his countrymen, or something more?

THE GREAT EMANCIPATOR is the story of a simple man. Born in the wilds of Kentucky and mostly self taught, Abraham Lincoln would someday be regarded as the greatest American who ever lived.

THE BULL MOOSE who occupied the White House 100 years ago was truly a man of action. Theodore Roosevelt was a father, author, rancher, sportsman, policeman, Rough Rider, cowboy, big game hunter, Governor of New York and eventually The President of the United States!

NIXON AND THE GHOSTS is a surreal drama with dialogue ripped straight from the headlines. On the night before his resignation, Nixon ponders his rise and fall, as the shadows themselves seem to come alive and he is confronted by the spirits of Presidents past!

NOW AVAILABLE!!!

The lights rise on a beautiful sunset.
A mermaid is silhouetted against an ocean backdrop.
Hauntingly familiar music fills the air.
Then...the Lawyer shows up.
And that's when the fun really begins!
The Little Mermaid (More or Less.) is the story of a Theatre company attempting to stage a children's version of the Hans Christian Anderson classic. The only problem? It looks and sounds an awful lot like a movie of the same name. That's when the Lawyer for a certain "mouse eared company" starts talking lawsuit for copyright infringement.
Lawsuit?
Copyright infringement?
Throw out the costumes!
What's that? There's a bunch of old clothes backstage from the 1970's? Well, don't just stand there! Go get them!
Ditch the music!
What? Somebody's mom has a greatest disco hits cd out in the car? That'll be perfect!
Change everyone's names!
Tartar Sauce! Little M.! The Crab Formerly Known as Sebastian!
Everybody ready? Ok...Action!!!

NOW AVAILABLE!!!

Adventure has a new name...

CINDERELLA!!!

Cinderella and the Quest for the Crystal Pump, is the story of a young girl seeking a life beyond the endless chores heaped upon her by her grouchy stepmother and two stepsisters.

Mow the grass! Beat the rugs! Churn the buttermilk!

Sometimes it's more than one girl can take!
More than anything, Cinderella wants to go to the prince's masquerade ball, but there's one problem...she has nothing to wear! Luckily, her Fairy Godperson has a few ideas.

Meanwhile, Prince Charles Edward Tiberius Charming III, or "Charlie" as he prefers to be called, has run away with his pals, Touchstone the Jester and the Magic Mirror, searching for a quiet place where he can just enjoy a good book!

Now this mismatched quartet find themselves on a quest to find the greatest treasure of all...the perfect pair of Crystal Pumps!

NOW AVAILABLE!!!

Everyone has heard the phrase, "it's the squeaky wheel that gets the oil," but how many people know the Back-story? The story begins in a kingdom far, far away over the rainbow – a kingdom called Spokend. This kingdom of wheels is a happy one for the gods have blessed the tiny hamlet with plentiful sunshine, water and most important –oil. Until a terrible drought starts to dry up all the oil supplies. What is to be done?

The powerful barons of industry and politicians decide to hold a meeting to decide how to solve the situation. Since Spokend is a democracy all the citizens come to the meeting but their voices are ignored – especially the voice of one of the poorer citizens of the community suffering from a squeak that can only be cured with oil, Spare Wheel and his wife Fifth Wheel. Despite Spare Wheel's desperate pleas for oil, he is ignored and sent home without any help or consideration.

Without oil, Spare Wheel's squeak becomes so bad he loses his job and his family starts to suffer when his sick leave and unemployment benefits run out. What is he to do? Spare Wheel and Fifth Wheel develop a scheme that uses the squeak to their advantage against the town magistrate Big Wheel who finally relents and gives over the oil. Thus, for years after in the town of Spokend citizens in need of help are told "It's the squeaky wheel that gets the oil."

www.ingramcontent.com/pod-product-compliance
Lightning Source LLC
Chambersburg PA
CBHW060703030426
42337CB00017B/2735